Tim Stafford

BROKE STAY BROKE

Copyright © Tim Stafford, 2025

All rights reserved. No part of this book may be used, performed, or reproduced in any manner whatsoever without written permission from the publisher except in the case of brief quotations embodied in critical articles or reviews.

First edition
ISBN: 978-1-949342-72-7

Cover Design by Jourdon Gullett
Interior Layout by Arkadii Pankevich
Edited by Haley Hutchinson, Adrian Wyatt
Author Photo by Hiu To

Type set in Bergamo

Printed in the USA

Write Bloody Publishing
Los Angeles, CA

Support Independent Presses
writebloody.com

Broke Stay Broke

ಌ

by Tim Stafford

Write Bloody

America's Independent Press

Los Angeles, CA

www.writebloody.com

*This Book is Dedicated
to my Dad, Michael W. Stafford
and my son, Michael L. Stafford*

TABLE OF CONTENTS

Part 1. Broke Stay Broke 9

    When You Are Broke 10
    The Financial Planner Says I'm Poor Because I Buy Coffee 12
    The Financial Planner Tells Us To Save for a Rainy Day and
        I Have Become a Civil War Soldier Stranded in a Flood
        Writing to His Beloved 14
    Broke Like 15
    Patient's Choice 16
    Benediction for When My Mechanic Calls to Tell Me
        What is Wrong With My Car 17
    Check Engine Light 18
    What My Dentist Sees When He Looks in My Mouth 19
    My Payment From a University Reading
        I Did 5 Months Ago Speaks 20
    When That Check Hits Tho… 21

Part 2. Broke Born Broke 23

    The Showcase Showdown 24
    Marlboro Miles 26
    4th of July: Hammond, Indiana 27
    Scratch Off 28
    Ode to the Cheater Box 29
    Mom in the Kitchen Baking a Penis Cake 30
    If My Mom Married Bruce Springsteen I Wouldn't Have
        to Deal With This Shit: Christmas, 1986 32
    A Dozen (or so)
        Half-Naked Polish Men 34
    Why We Got Kicked Out of the Taco Bell 36

Part 3. Rich Stay Rich 37

    Rich in the Winter 38
    Rich in the Spring 40
    Rules for Attending Parties in the Homes of Old Money 41
    What the Rich Kids Complained About, I Wanted 43

    Tiny Disasters 44
    One of Them Jobs 46

Part 4. A Couple of Poems For My Pal Shappy Whom I Miss Very Much............................. 49

    When I'm Sad I Pretend You Moved Back
        to Astoria, Queens 50
    Barnes Foundation, Philadelphia 52

Part 5. Poems for My Loved Ones. Poems for Chicago 53

    Meet Me at O'Hare and Tell Me You Love Me 54
    A Quarantine Poem About Missing My Friends 55
    For the Health of My Son............................... 56
    Big Shot at the Green Mill 57
    Closest I've Been to Venice............................. 58
    WILCO Dads.. 60

Part 6. Broke Boy's Guide to Travel 63

    Never Been to Rome 64
    Ode to TSA Precheck................................... 65
    The Skateboarders of Taos, New Mexico................ 66
    Apologies to Lübeck 68

Part 7. Broke Still Broke (But Getting Better) 71

    When You're Not That Broke Anymore 72
    Elegy for a Closed Credit Card.......................... 73
    When a Student Asks Me if I Would Quit Teaching
        if I Became Rich..................................... 74
    List of Things I Will Try To Use as Tax Write-Offs......... 75
    Hundred Dollar Handshake 76
    What I Really Want 77
    We Still Tip the Wait Staff at Least 20 Percent 79
    Dreams Ain't Fun No More............................. 80

Epilogue... 82

About the Author 84

Acknowledgments 85

Thank you 86

PART 1

BROKE STAY BROKE

WHEN YOU ARE BROKE

1.

You are the Bob Fosse of financial illiteracy
a master choreographer the way you maneuver
your credit cards in and out of rotation
to avoid overages, late fees, more hits
to your credit score.

Your credit score
is steadily
tap-dancing
toward oblivion.

2.

You are a Twilight Zone episode
no one wants to watch.

The way every route mapped
to lead you out of distress
loops back to where you started.

3.

You are the Miss Cleo of decision-making
the world's worst psychic
the way you already know how bad
this decision will affect you in the long term
but you make it anyway.

There is no down payment
only a minimum payment.

4.

You are a professional defeatist
and you have to win
all of the grants,
all of the prizes,
all of the awards,
to pay off your debts.

So you apply to none.

THE FINANCIAL PLANNER SAYS I'M POOR BECAUSE I BUY COFFEE

Were you aware that if you stop
buying coffee for a week you
will have enough money to get
your teeth fixed?

If you stop buying coffee
for a month, you could afford
that vacation to Rome you've
always dreamed of—

If you stop buying coffee
for six months you will create
enough generational wealth
that none of your offspring
will ever need to work, ever—

If you stop buying coffee
for a year you can purchase
a dunk tank filled with
molten gold—

Stop buying coffee
for two years and you
can place your enemies
in the dunk tank
entomb them in 14 Karat
display them in the sculpture
garden amongst your collection
of Koons' and Rodin's—

Stop buying coffee
for three years and you'll
be able to pay off the
detectives, jury and judge
all murder charges dismissed
causing a spike in the value
of your murder statues
turning you into the
richest man who will
ever walk the Earth—

It's basic economics.

THE FINANCIAL PLANNER TELLS US TO SAVE FOR A RAINY DAY AND I HAVE BECOME A CIVIL WAR SOLDIER STRANDED IN A FLOOD WRITING TO HIS BELOVED

My Dearest Abigail,

I have been clinging to the detritus of what was once our home for nearly a fortnight. My only source of comfort is the hundreds of men staying afloat on tables and doors lashed together with lace curtains that once hung proudly in the parlors and grand dining rooms of our beloved homeland. We are a flotilla of lost souls set adrift in these unholy waters. Our hopes for survival rise and fall with the waves. O Abigail, how every breeze that tickles my skin reminds me of your touch. I yearn, nay, I desire, nothing more than to lay my eyes upon you one last time before the current takes me home to the Creator. My only consolation is knowing the raindrops that leak from this evil sky hide the traces of my tears. If I can ask you for one thing, it would be to forget me. Do not allow my memory to become a burden. Go forth and be merry. Find a husband who is a peaceable man. Find a husband who acknowledges flash flood warnings and seeks higher ground. But don't marry Jimmy. You know Jimmy? The financial planner with the khakis creased so tight they could cut through butter? Fuck that guy.

Drenched,
Private Harrison Ambrose McGillicuddy

BROKE LIKE

Broke like the iPhone
I dropped in the toilet
at work while checking my
email for word about the new job:

> The one with a living wage
> and health insurance
> The one I was supposed to hear
> back from last week

Broke like when I
tried to get the same
model of iPhone and
was informed they
stopped making that
model three years ago

Broke like when I realized
my old iPhone was purchased
seven years ago

before the divorce and
the debt accumulated
like unanswered emails and
text messages asking me
why I don't go out anymore

At least now I have an excuse
for never responding

PATIENT'S CHOICE

Sitting on a bench in
the West Loop watching
folks who can afford to
live in the West Loop walk
hypoallergenic dogs that
cost more than my car

Waiting for the part-time
gig that was supposed to
be a temporary gig but
has now morphed into
the absolutely necessary gig

Hoping the novocain
from my dentist appointment
between the full-time gig
and the part-time gig
doesn't wear off until
my shift is over

My dentist told me the cost
of repair or a pull and
allowed me to make
the decision though
he knows how much
I do not have

Which is why I sit here with
gauze stuffed into the void

Counting how many more
shifts I will need to work
to pay off my balance

BENEDICTION FOR WHEN MY MECHANIC CALLS TO TELL ME WHAT IS WRONG WITH MY CAR

Lord, first we ask for longevity:
that the diagnosis is not terminal
that the damage is repairable
that the car can last
      for another year
            hopefully, two

Lord, next we ask for compassion:
that his knowledge of mechanical
      engineering be surpassed only
           by his empathy
that he find a used replacement
      part in the back
that he knock off a couple of bucks
      for being a valued customer
that he throws in an oil change
      or a hug

And lastly, Lord, we pray for my finances:
that the estimate is not panic-inducing
that the repairs stay in the low three-figures
that the immediate repairs be covered
      by the part-time check
that the rest fade
      from our memories.

CHECK ENGINE LIGHT

My check engine light glows
like a log pulled from a bonfire
which is an inappropriate simile
considering the heat in my
car does not work.

WHAT MY DENTIST SEES WHEN HE LOOKS IN MY MOUTH

He is a rapper from the early
2000s starring in his own video
soaking in a jacuzzi filled
with champagne which can't
be good for the skin
but is excellent
for his reputation.

The jacuzzi is on the back
of a yacht. A big one.
The scope of which can only
be appreciated with a wide shot
taken from a helicopter
that swoops in close.

Close enough to make
his unbuttoned Versace
blouse flap wildly.
Close enough
to make his hangers-on stuff
their ears with caviar
to block the noise.

He's got so much ice
he's worried about frostbite.
Afraid he might go blind
from the shine of the diamond-
encrusted saliva ejector
hanging off his necklace.

He doesn't make me say *Ahhhh* anymore, no
he makes me say *Uhh! Na, Nah, Na, Nah.*

MY PAYMENT FROM A UNIVERSITY READING I DID 5 MONTHS AGO SPEAKS

Have you ever been to Paris in the Spring?
Ever sit at an outdoor cafe, the late morning
sun allowing a loosening of the scarf
a slight, steady breeze cooling your
cappuccino to sippable warmth?

There is something about watching
the final clumps of snow release their grip
on the cobblestone walkways, drain
themselves into the Seine, and wait to
be reborn as fog rolling off the English Channel.

I am much like those snow clumps:

    patient
        endless

            and nowhere
            near your mailbox

WHEN THAT CHECK HITS THO…

It's a party
it's a fucking festival
I take the past due notices
that have stacked up on
my kitchen table like a
monument to my fiscal
irresponsibility and shred them
Throw a ticker tape
parade in my honor
because I fucking made it
through another month
Phone bill? Paid
ComEd? Paid
Minimum payments on
all four credit cards?
GET OFF MY BACK!
The crowd roars when
they see me invest in
the 12-pack of razors
instead of the 4-pack
The crowd explodes when
they see me buy toilet paper
The good kind! In bulk!
Enough to keep us
wiped right for weeks!
Next month is next month's problem
because right now I am light
I am a float
I am a parade balloon
pumped full of helium
drifting down State St.
The handlers can't keep
hold of the ropes and
everything is going up, up, up—

PART 2

BROKE BORN BROKE

THE SHOWCASE SHOWDOWN

He watched every morning
pictured himself riding one of
the his-and-hers wave runners
out of our town and straight
into high society.

Once there, he would regale
his new friends with tales
from his all-expenses-paid
trip to Greece leaving out
the part where he lived off the
free toast and jam he saved
from the hotel breakfast,
the only free meal included
in the package.

How long could he
wear the diamond tennis
bracelet before an
invitation to play at
the country club?

How long could his
Chevy Cavalier
look showroom ready
before the neighbors
started to notice the
tell-tale signs of
daily use?

What if his rich friends
watch the Price is Right
to make fun of poor people
wildly gesticulating at the

prospect of winning furniture
that would not fit into their
one-bedroom apartment?

Would they recognize him
in his homemade sweater,
the one with "I Love Bob"
written in gold puffy paint,
his first name plastered
on a name tag for all to see?

Maybe they'd be impressed
he guessed the Showcase
within $500.

Maybe they'd hire him
to be a price analyst
which is a job he
is not sure exists but
sounds real enough.

Maybe like a Plinko
chip pinging from side
to side he'd land in
the jackpot slot, be
allowed to stay.

Every day he'd watch
and tell us about his plans
to take his dad's 1989
Geo Storm, drive out to Burbank
leaving us all behind.

We knew two things:
That car wouldn't make it
to the state line and even if
it could, he'd never
leave the block.

MARLBORO MILES

A kid on my block got
a Marlboro leather jacket
in the mail and he
was a god.

Measured his life
in Marlboro miles
torn from the back
of packs

purchased at
the bowling alley
the convenience store
the Amoco station

wherever didn't card hard
or at all
or still accepted notes from aunts
or had an unguarded vending machine.

A latch-key kid with a pack-
a-day habit in the seventh grade
though he was held back in first
but still, that's commitment.

Walked to school smelling
like a strip club couch
all leather and smoke
and Cool Water cologne

would hotbox the loosie
tucked behind his ear before
entering school, saying hello
to his principal

who wouldn't dare ask
him to take it off.

4TH OF JULY: HAMMOND, INDIANA

There are a million ways
to blow off your fingers
and you can find them all
at Krazy Kaplan's Fireworks

Families spend what they do not have
on pyrotechnics because they gonna
be hungry anyway so why not blow some
shit up to feel something and give the kids
something to remember, something to
talk about when they go back to school
and the others speak of trips to
Wisconsin Dells or Disney

Oh, you saw Mickey Mouse?
I saw my Dad light a 5" Raging Bull
mortar shell with his bare hands
and throw it like he was still
on the high school baseball team.
Chucked that motherfucker
over the heads of friends and
family gathered in folding chairs
like it was a grenade because it was

Sparks trailing down
like a dare to try again
until he ran out of fireworks
or beer, until the cops show up
the guests scattering like
a pack of Jumping Jacks
left too close to the ashtray

SCRATCH OFF

Everyone knows a guy
whose cousin worked
for a woman whose
nephew won seventy-five
thousand dollars from
a scratch-off ticket.

Got those three
treasure chests
or a triple bonus
on twenty-five

cashed it in and lived
ignorantly until it evaporated
like the water in the jacuzzi
he installed on his new deck.

It's a shame what happened,
folks said as his new car
rolled down the street on
the back of a tow truck.

It's a shame, they said
as the jacuzzi
the leather sectional
with the built-in sound system
were repossessed.

When it was all gone
and all debts were settled
he'd walk down the street
to catch the bus to work

he'd smile at his neighbors
who never won nothing
knowing that he was at
least a winner once

ODE TO THE CHEATER BOX

How many drunk uncles,
neighbors, coworkers, etc
can you fit into a basement
to watch Tyson destroy some
fool in less than a minute?

The answer is all of them

if your Dad knew a guy
or if he lucked out with a
cable installer working
a side hustle.

You descrambler of despair

The FCC got nothing on
these clandestine gatherings
of working stiffs who know how
to enjoy something without asking
too many questions

You liberator of the Pay Per View

folks who can't afford
the good life will soak up
as much as they can before
retreating to their basic
cable existence.

MOM IN THE KITCHEN BAKING A PENIS CAKE

We have been banished to our bedrooms
as our Mom bakes a cake in solitude

Our Mom, the president of the Society
of Catholic Women, bakes often

Never at night

Mostly for others
and not for too much
Enough to take the edge
off the grocery bill

For the right price, she could make
a 3-D graduation cap with a cake base
and cookie mortarboard

She could make a teddy bear so
realistic the birthday kid would
cry when it was cut

Graduations
Birthdays
First Communions
and Tonight
for the first and last time
a Bachelorette Party

Tonight she will not let us fill the cake pan
with batter as silky as the pope's
Easter vestments

She will not let us mix food coloring
into the vat of white icing

She will definitely not let us
lick the batter from the beaters

The cake iced peach
Her cheeks flushed red

Thinking of how she'll
confess to this

Hoping the confessional screen
is thick enough to hide her smile

IF MY MOM MARRIED BRUCE SPRINGSTEEN I WOULDN'T HAVE TO DEAL WITH THIS SHIT: CHRISTMAS, 1986

My Dad is the manager
of Dominick's Finer Foods
but he is not The Boss

He does not play guitar in a band
with his friend Clarence Carter
that became critical darlings
before breaking through
to mainstream success

He plays horseshoes in a league
with his friend Harvey that
had to shut down mid-season
because the league president
took off with the prize money

Bruce Springsteen
would not let that happen

Even if it did
Bruce would write a song about it
maybe headline a benefit show
until all the money was paid back
or he would just pay for it himself

You know what else Bruce Springsteen
wouldn't mind paying for? A new skateboard.
A real one instead of the rip-off
from the department store

that weighs thirty pounds and
rolls three inches unlike
the Mike McGill pro-model
from the back of Thrasher magazine
that was circled in red marker with a note
attached that read "BUY THIS ONE"
with arrows pointing to all the
information needed to procure
such an item

Mom, you could do better.

A DOZEN (OR SO) HALF-NAKED POLISH MEN

A dozen or so half-naked Polish men
were living in my neighbor's basement.

My brother spotted them through
the only basement window not
covered in cardboard.

The dozen or so half-naked Polish men
slept on cots lined up on the basement floor.

It reminded me of the WGN news
reporting from a gymnasium filled with
families displaced by tornado strikes.

Only these cots were filled with
a dozen or so half-naked Polish men.

Some of them wandered to unseen parts
of the basement in only white briefs
whose elastic waistbands stretched
to the limit by their expansive stomachs.

As if the further they stuck out
would be that much less distance
between them and their families.

We told our Dad who says he knows.
He's seen them in the early morning

fully-clothed

hurrying into the back of a windowless
panel van emblazoned with the name
of our neighbor's construction company.

We asked him who they were.
He said they were here illegally
saving up money for family back home
or until they could get green cards
or for any reason we were born
privileged enough not to fathom.

If they are illegal, we ask,
shouldn't you call the cops?
Maybe, he says, maybe.

The sirens never screamed down our street.
The news never showed images of
a dozen or so half-naked Polish men
handcuffed in the back of a paddy wagon.

It was the only business lesson
our Dad ever taught us:

to mind our own.

WHY WE GOT KICKED OUT OF THE TACO BELL

It wasn't because we were skateboarding in their parking lot, it was because we kept going back with the same cup well past the unspoken limit of free refills and we could get away with that shit when the girl who wore the Operation Ivy pin on her apron was working the counter but Carl was working that day and Carl was one of those sad assholes who bought into the Taco Bell corporate structure and he truly thought he would move from the counter to becoming an owner one day even though he would have to work 200 hours a week for a thousand years to afford the franchise fee so when we took advantage of the free refill policy he took it as a personal affront and chased us out of the parking lot but he didn't see us drive my Grandma's minivan around the block, nor did he see the sliding door open up so John could jump out, steal a chair from the dining room and get back in faster than Carl could say Chilito which used to be on the menu before they changed it to a Chili Cheese Burrito, before they took it off the menu entirely, and we drove off with our turquoise trophy which I held onto for 20 years until I put in my kid's room and now he sits on it while he draws monsters and sharks and shit.

PART 3

RICH STAY RICH

RICH IN THE WINTER

I want enough money to fight God.
Enough money to laugh at
their attempts to hurt me, to slap
me with the sting of winter.

My floors, heated.
My car, heated.
My coat, chinchilla
or something else
cute and nearly extinct.

Someone poorer than me
will shovel and salt
my sidewalk
my walkway
my driveway—

My shoes, stitched together
by Italian cobblers from a
village they will never visit,
will touch neither
snow nor salt.

Partly because I only hire the best
but mostly because
I won't even
be home.

I'll be on a private beach
on a private island
in another home
because I've got
it like that.

Jealous?

Should've thought about
that before you took
out those student loans.

At least you can burn
all of the past-due notices
to keep warm.

RICH IN THE SPRING

Spring Break is whenever and
for however long I want it to be

Puerto Vallarta? Cabo? Cancun?
Why not all three?

Perhaps I will parasail over the public
beaches but not step on them

Perhaps I will hook a marlin
the size of a Subaru

Perhaps I will scream at the woman
behind the car rental desk when
she hands me the keys to a Subaru
when I specifically asked for a
BMW Series 3 or something similar

Perhaps I will ask her if she knows
who I am and the power I yield
I will be shocked when
she tells me she has no idea
who I am nor does she care

Perhaps I will spend the
rest of the evening crying
in my Presidential Suite
questioning the meaning of
acquired wealth and its inability
to make me feel whole

Not only do 1,000 thread count
Egyptian sheets provide comfort
they are surprisingly efficient
at wiping away my tears

RULES FOR ATTENDING PARTIES IN THE HOMES OF OLD MONEY

Keep your cool while attending
parties in the homes of old money.

Do not gawk at the one-of-a-kind,
museum-worthy furniture.

Pay no attention to the chaise lounge carved
from a single piece of mahogany

by a blind woodworker in Latvia
who only makes one piece per year.

Do not ask about the price
or where they got it from.

Such inquiries are tacky,
unbecoming to those in the know.

Instead, regard the furniture
as you would a park bench.

They are not for sitting.
They are made for admiring
so admire it. From afar.

While attending a party in
a home of old money

be sure to steal something.
An ashtray, a glass figurine.

Something small that won't be
noticed for some time.

Something you do not need but
that is not the point. Just take it.

Be sure to bring the stolen
object with you

when you attend another party
in a different home of old money.

Place the purloined item in a
high traffic, high visibility area.

Watch as the rightful owners
recognize their lost possession.

Watch as they play out
scenarios in their mind,

surmising that anyone capable
of theft is capable of anything.

What's next?
Kidnapping?
Murder?

When you attend a party in
a home of old money

be sure to try the liver pâté.
It is divine.

WHAT THE RICH KIDS COMPLAINED ABOUT, I WANTED

Spanish classes
in Barcelona

Weekends
at the family lake house

A flight
to London
in coach

The right car
The wrong color

A housekeeper who
goes through my stuff
and snitches to my parents

Parents who love me
enough to leave me

Money for a week's
worth of takeout
but not enough
to take me with them
on vacation

TINY DISASTERS

My supervisor got
ten-thousand dollars for
getting his foot run over
by a taxi cab.

Broken in one place.
Six weeks on crutches.
Paid leave.
Good as new.

Got me wondering
about the worth
of my own body.
Of what I'd be willing to
give up and for
what price.

A broken leg must be worth
at least twenty-thousand.
Double the time to heal but
double the time off.

And what of these toes?
Maybe I should start with those.
What could I get for a pinky
cleaved straight off
my right foot?

Slight mangling via street sweeper.
Non-life-threatening mutilation
by garbage truck.
Low-key disfigurement.

Who needs all those piggies?
Who needs all these fingers?
Not all of them of course.
A couple from the left hand.

I'd hire one of those lawyers
with the late-night commercials
and the billboards as large
as the check they'd win me.

I could send my kid to
college for a couple digits.
Have enough left for a car
that starts. All the time.

My supervisor didn't
even need the money.
Paid for the golf trip he
had already planned.

Bought himself a
new set of clubs that
looked like they were
from the future.

Built of lightweight
titanium like the pins
I'd be willing to put
in my rebuilt femur.

But here I stand.
Woefully intact.
Dangling my feet
from the curb.

Fishing for
a tiny disaster
to call my own.

ONE OF THEM JOBS

I want one of them jobs
The kind with signing bonuses
and matched 401K's

The kind of job where people
brainstorm ideas on glass walls
with neon markers and call it
"spitballing"

Everyone wears jeans and blazers
with graphic t-shirts underneath
and calls themselves "disruptors"

There's a keg of beer in the
break room because the boss
is a cool boss who wants everyone
to work hard and play hard

Which is weird because at the
Christmas party last year Jake
in the graphics department got fired
for spiking the dunk tank with LSD

Made everyone think a giant snake
was loose in the building and their
open-office concept offered no
protection from its wrath

Julie from HR passed out after looking
in the mirror and seeing her fresh blowout
transform into a nest of vipers that
would make Medusa proud

Amir from Marketing called his mom to say
good-bye before he was swallowed whole
Said he could feel its jaws tightening around
his ankles but really it was just fresh elastic
in his designer joggers

Dale in Sales drop-kicked his assistant
because he thought they were turning
into an anaconda but the whole office
knows Dale's been wanting to drop-kick
his assistant ever since they popped-out
in the final at-bat of the kickball tournament

Jake didn't kill anyone but he did kill
the vibe for the annual karaoke contest

The one time of year when the Boss dusts off
the mic and offers an unironic rendition of "Sussudio"
to inspire their employees to a successful
and profitable Quarter one

For that, Jake had to be released with
full severance package including extended
healthcare, three months pay, and a letter
of recommendation in exchange for a signed NDA

I want one of them jobs
Where do I apply?

PART 4

A COUPLE OF POEMS FOR MY PAL SHAPPY WHOM I MISS VERY MUCH

WHEN I'M SAD I PRETEND YOU MOVED BACK TO ASTORIA, QUEENS

FedEx just delivered
a box full of not particularly
rare or sought-after
Happy Meal toys while
your girlfriend is at work
which leaves you enough
time to hide them from her
like a junkie that gets high
off molded plastic
and nostalgia.

You carry your laundry
in a bulging sack like Santa
if kids asked Santa for V-neck
sweaters and Hawaiian shirts
and drop it off at that
spot down the block,
rewarding yourself with
a visit to the comic shop
where you announce your
arrival and everyone knows
your name.

It's not Tuesday so you leave
empty-handed except
for the free alt-weekly
tucked under your armpit,
something to pass the
time with while you
wait for your meal in a
booth upholstered
to look like a scallop shell.

You are a Botticelli in cargo shorts,
a schmeer of cream cheese
on your chin.

BARNES FOUNDATION, PHILADELPHIA

I dreamed about you
sitting at a long table
hewn from a single
piece of extinct timber
amongst the items
your friends had gathered:

> Cracked CD cases
> Tattered composition books
> Journals sheathed in Star Wars stickers

A stack of VHS tapes
obstructed my view
but I knew it was you

reading through your
work and belly-laughing
at your own brilliance,
laughter that poured
through every corridor
into every gallery

I was really
fucking good,

you said to
Van Gogh's "Postman"
that hung to your left

A silent agreement
between two masters
underappreciated in
their time

PART 5

POEMS FOR MY LOVED ONES. POEMS FOR CHICAGO

MEET ME AT O'HARE AND TELL ME YOU LOVE ME

For Hiu

You gave up driving like
eating meat and casual drug use

This means you rode
a couple of busses to take the
Blue Line the hard way

You carry no signs
no balloons just an
offer to take a bag
so I can drink the coffee
you've been holding
since Damen Ave.

Still warm

You don't tell me you love me
but your Ventra card has
enough train fare for two
and isn't that the same thing?

A QUARANTINE POEM ABOUT MISSING MY FRIENDS

"I dream of this. Hanging out. I dream of hanging out."
- Action Bronson

That's it right?
To linger.
To keep company.
To shoot the shit.
To listen to another record.
To order another round
at the corner bar.
On a stoop.
On a rooftop.
On a deck the landlord
claims is up to code
despite the chorus of
creaks with every step.
Probably at a kitchen table
pretending we haven't
heard the same stories.
Had the same arguments.
Details changing and fading.
Some lost altogether.
I should have gone home
an hour ago but we haven't
been in the same room
since the baby was born.
Or the promotion was achieved.
Or the divorce was finalized.
And I don't know when we'll pull this
off again so somebody please
put on a fresh pot of coffee
because I got dirt on all
these assholes and tonight
I will make the time.

FOR THE HEALTH OF MY SON

For Michael

Let my teeth crumble into dusty heaps
        my eyes bulge from
        their sockets to the
        point of bursting

I will trade all ten fingers
        all ten toes
an eyeball
my sense of smell

Take my hair
        or give me too much
        make me a sasquatch
        a bearded lady

Give me a horn that grows
        from the middle of my forehead
        over my nose
        down to my chin

I will be a medical oddity
        examined and hypothesized
        articles published in journals
        about my condition

And upon my death
        have me stuffed
        put on display
        charge admission

Let my son keep the fee

BIG SHOT AT THE GREEN MILL

He shakes my hand with a grip so tight
it hurts my feelings

The owner knows me but I'm
not sure if he knows my name

With a Chicago accent heavier than
a breaded steak sandwich he says,

Hey there, Fucker!

He shows me to an open booth
and doesn't let me pay for drinks

I say it's because he values
my artistic contributions

My girl says it's because
I only drink sodas or seltzer

I tell her that jealousy is not
a good look for her

And that is why there are now
two people who I hold dear

who call me "Fucker"

CLOSEST I'VE BEEN TO VENICE

A late-night open mic ain't
that bad if you don't have to
work the next day and you
are in your twenties

And you don't feel bad
inviting your friends who
showed up because no one
is close to having kids

And if you're lucky J will
show up with an accordion
gifted to him by garbage
or by grace

He won't bring it for the open mic
He'll bring it because he's a
musical savant who can learn
an instrument by running
his fingers over the keys
and buttons

That doesn't make any sense
except it will work and by the time
we leave the venue with enough
money for the train or a couple of drinks
J has figured it out

He'll squeeze out an Italian number
that bounces off the brick three-flats
and lingers like our breath in the
late November air

They say Italian is the language of love
but I have to disagree

It is a mother with a Chicago accent
calling out from her frunchroom
to tell him to knock that shit off
because her kids are trying to sleep

WILCO DADS

They have tattoos of the Chicago flag
to commemorate their life-long
dedication to the city they lived in
for the two years they spent at DePaul
getting their Master's Degree in
some kind of finance before moving
back to the suburbs
whence they came

or River North

They will ask you what music you listen to
and no matter your answer will reply,
If you like that, you'll probably like WILCO

They talk about WILCO
as if WILCO were an underground
sensation you could hear only
at secret shows in the darkest
nooks of Lower Wacker Drive

WILCO Dads eat edibles before school functions
and let everyone know they ate edibles
before the school function

At the school function they will
find other WILCO Dads wearing
their WILCO shirts and list every
WILCO show they've been to and if
another WILCO Dad was at
the same WILCO show they
will high-five, they will hug

They will hold each other's gaze
They will imagine a life together
based around the music and lyrics of WILCO

There will be WILCO concerts
There will be framed, limited edition silk-screened
posters of those concerts that their wives would
not let them hang in the living room amongst the
family photos but there are no wives in
the WILCO World
No kids either
Kids these days don't like WILCO
Kids don't understand the genius of WILCO
even though their WILCO Dad would
play WILCO albums on the way to school
and try to explain to them why this droning
15-minute song is actually a metaphor
for the lead singer's migraines and drug addiction
so it's supposed to sound like shit

The edibles will wear off
WILCO World will dissolve into
the real world where the WILCO Dads
are loved by their children
tolerated by their wives
their dogs are indifferent
and Jeff Tweedy is still trying
to break their hearts

PART 6

BROKE BOY'S GUIDE TO TRAVEL

NEVER BEEN TO ROME

But I thought I was going
to get murdered in Hamburg
by soccer thugs with necks
thick as stacked tires

Ended up with benevolent
locals who spirited us to
to a rusty park in a sketchy
area overlooking the port

With friends who I
love very much but
haven't seen since that night

Maybe they're still there
drinking bottles of cheap wine
watching cranes lifting cargo
as if on marionette strings

ODE TO TSA PRECHECK

I know you are curious about
what kind of liquids are in my bag
but you know a little mystery helps
keep the spark alive.

You don't need to see my laptop
because our relationship is
based on trust.

You let me keep all my clothes on
and it is somehow sexier.

I love you the way Delta loves
canceling flights for no reason.

I love you like my Dad loves showing
up to the airport three hours early
for a domestic flight.

I will abandon my wife to
the shoeless ne'er do wells
and ragamuffins of the hellscape
of regular security just to
spend a couple of minutes with you.

What I'm trying to say is
we go together like Hudson News
and fifteen-dollar bags of chips.

THE SKATEBOARDERS
OF TAOS, NEW MEXICO

Down in the plaza
a cacophony of failed kickflips
echoed off the adobe facades of the
closed gift shops and cowboy stores.

I could see them from
the window of my room.

I paid extra for the privilege
of a plaza-facing room because I
could afford it but I wasn't
sure for how long.

I could see them
but I didn't.

Writhing instead on the bathroom
floor, the tiles cooling my back,
leaking sweat thanks to a
food poisoning-induced fever.

Between my bouts of purging,
amidst the chatter, the clicks,
the pops, I heard them clapping
and cheering

which meant someone
either landed a difficult trick
or someone landed a new trick
they'd been working on
for days.

I like to think they were clapping for me
cheering for me, a grown man more than
double their age, shivering on a
bathroom floor who gave up on
kickflips years ago.

APOLOGIES TO LÜBECK

for Björn and Tilo

When given the choice
between a bar with women
or a bar that serves whiskey
we chose whiskey
because in Lübeck, Germany
you cannot have both

It was a jazz bar named
after a Russian painter
that played British heavy metal

My travel companions and I
had made a pact:
We would not be the loud Americans
We would be polite
We would be courteous
We would not wear out our welcome

And we were

We were downright diplomatic
Goodwill ambassadors with
questionable beards
and dumb haircuts

We sipped our drinks slowly and smoked
our cigarettes in drags
as long as the legs of the women
who were not in this bar

Our nonexistent German
ensured that conversation flowed
like the shower drain in our hostel
that hadn't been cleaned for weeks

My fellow Americans
were now sounding
more like Americans

The Germans were now sounding
more like Americans because
closing Time is a universal language.
We rolled out like a rockslide onto
the ancient cobblestone

Strutted down the narrow
streets belting "Living on a Prayer"
as if it was the Star Spangled Banner
Our voices shooting off like Patriot missiles
till we crash landed in our hostel
weighed down by jet lag, alcohol, life,
liberty, and the pursuit of happiness

Lübeck: We are so sorry
that we were so awesome that night

We are the reason your citizens
started wearing backwards baseball caps
and watching monster truck races

We are the reason they are overweight
because these colors?
They do not run.

PART 7:

BROKE STILL BROKE (BUT GETTING BETTER)

WHEN YOU'RE NOT THAT BROKE ANYMORE

You have built yourself a castle
with walls ten feet thick with stone
and a moat full of underfed alligators
archers perched on each parapet
cauldrons of skin-stripping oil
waiting above the drawbridge
in case of a breach

You still wake up in pitch-black
expecting to see your enemies
scaling the ramparts
the glint of torches reflecting
off the blades in their teeth

If they don't come over the walls
they'll come through them
and you can't see the trebuchets
marshaled along the tree line
but you can feel them
projectiles loaded
ropes pulled taut
aimed

All you can do is wait around
for the counterweight to drop

ELEGY FOR A CLOSED CREDIT CARD

I still feel you like a phantom limb
throbbing in my back pocket every time
I get gas or walk by a coffee shop
serving artisanal pastries

I reach back for you the same way
I had when I met friends for dinner
and even though I showed up late
and indulged in neither appetizer
nor drink they wanted to split the check

I reach back for you the same way
I had done every 16th of the month
to make your payment in time
holding my breath while the automaton
announced your balance that grew
like my waistline thanks to the coffee shop
that serves artisanal pastries

I reach back for you but find
only an impression in my wallet

Maybe we will meet again when
I too experience zero utilization
when all debts personal and public
are paid in full and I am ready
to start
all over again

WHEN A STUDENT ASKS ME IF I WOULD QUIT TEACHING IF I BECAME RICH

Am I a short man?

Do you like to remind me
that I am a short man?

Do I stay up late at night
haunted by you and your
classmates' remarks about
my shoes and outfits?

Do I wish I had better shoes?

Do I wish I could afford
a decent outfit?

Do you act dumbfounded
when I tell you are failing
my class and when I offered
you make up work you told me,
I'm good fam?

Do you need to ask me
what dumbfounded means?

Would you like to rephrase
your question?

LIST OF THINGS I WILL TRY TO USE AS TAX WRITE-OFFS

1. The fifty dollars worth of gas I used
to get to the poetry gig that paid seventy-five

2. The coffee I bought on the way home
from that poetry gig because it was late
and I was tired from working all day
and the same student who makes short
jokes to me every day made a joke
that was actually funny but I had to
be an adult and not say anything
because I cannot afford to get fired
this close to Christmas which is why
I took this poetry gig in the first place

3. Blood-pressure medication

4. One gas station burrito because I like
to keep my blood pressure medication
on its toes

5. The group of teenagers who saw me
eat that burrito like I had been left for dead
in the wilderness and that burrito was
the first thing I had eaten in months
that was neither berry nor bug. They looked
at me with a mix of wonder, pity, and sadness,
the emotional toll it took on me is incalculable

6. Therapy

HUNDRED DOLLAR HANDSHAKE

Never a hundred-dollar bill
Mostly fives and singles

Enough to give the
wad some weight

It's less than what I need
but it's enough to keep on

Enough to fill in the blanks
on the grocery list

Enough for a Lego set for the kid
nothing too big

Enough to keep the illusion
of having my shit together

Until the day I can actually
get my shit together

WHAT I REALLY WANT

Is to not wait for the paperback edition

I want to walk into a bookstore and see
a display featuring the latest book
by my favorite author

Heavy, thick, hardcover

The kind of book that makes
you adjust your backpack straps

I want to pick it up
run my fingers over the dull ridges
of the embossed title on the dust jacket

I want to look at the inside flap
and not flinch when I see the price

To not worry if it will bust my budget

I want to worry only about whether
or not I can finish it before the
spoilers get leaked

I want to crack that spine
like a chiropractor

I want to read it by the light
of the fireplace in my library
amongst the shelves lined
with my collection of
hardcover books
all first-edition

I want a fireplace

I want a library

I want to sit

I want time

WE STILL TIP THE WAIT STAFF AT LEAST 20 PERCENT

We might be broke
We are not assholes

DREAMS AIN'T FUN NO MORE

1

My dreams are the color
of curbside slush

Every day is February
Everywhere is Indiana
Every bill is past due

My car is towed
My wallet is stolen
My passport is missing

I wake up with my heart making
blast beats against my sternum

2

When I tell you my dreams were the best
I mean my dreams were in technicolor
My dreams were tactile

They took place in cities made up
of the best parts of the best cities
I could hop on a bus in Budapest
get off at the next stop and be
in my mind's version of Kyoto

I performed at sold-out shows
I sold all of my books
I landed every trick on my skateboard
I found Basquiat paintings at thrift stores

My wallet was always fat
but nothing cost anything, anyway

My dead friends would meet me
at cafes and parks and libraries

They would guide me through
art museums, take pieces off the wall
and tell me, *You should have this*

I had a home with walls large
and open enough to hang the piece

We'd admire it while sipping coffee
that always stayed warm

3

My friends don't visit as much but
when they do, I can't see their faces
just blurs like an erased answer
from a Scantron bubble

They don't stay long

They wave from the other
side of the window and
disappear before I can
make my way out

But still, they come
They keep showing up

so I do too.

EPILOGUE

Hey Gang,

Most of these poems were written after the worst of my broke-ness. I'm not wealthy; my savings account has enough to buy a really nice cup of coffee, but I don't panic on the 15th of every month wondering how I'll make my credit card payments. I don't worry about ComEd sending goons to my house to break my legs. Somehow, I achieved this without starting my own LLC.

This is all to say, I sleep much better.

It took me a while to write this book because of the shame I felt about my financial standing. I had done everything I thought I was supposed to: go to college, buy a home, get a job, etc. I did not live extravagantly, I drove used cars, and I didn't do drugs. Yet every month I kept slipping a little further into debt. I did a good job of hiding it from people. If you were to look at my social media, I would seem like someone who had my shit together.

Now that I do have my shit together, I humbly offer some advice on how to become less broke.

Broke Boy's Guide to Being Less Broke

Look at the Numbers: I knew I was in debt, but I didn't realize to what extent until I ran a free credit report. There are many options, but I used the Credit Sesame app. It's free and very plainly showed me what I owed. It helped me prioritize my payments to cards with a higher rate and it showed me how to build up my credit score.

Be Patient: When possible, avoid short-term solutions that will bite you in the long run. I had an old 401K from a printing job right out of college. The amount was enough to pay off one of my credit cards. I was tempted to cash it in and thankfully I did not. I would have been penalized for cashing it in early and then I would have had to pay extra taxes on the amount. It wouldn't have been enough, and I would have missed out on the value it has accumulated since. Also, avoid payday loans like the plague.

Work, Work, Work, Work, Work: I worked a lot. In addition to my full-time job, I tutored, performed poetry, sold books, etc. I used sick days from my job to teach writing workshops wherever would pay me. It was exhausting but that extra cash would go straight to paying debt. I certainly hoped for a windfall whether it was a huge paying gig or an inheritance from a distant, rich relative I didn't know about. I hoped, but I kept working.

Drive a Shitty Car: Better yet, don't own a car at all. But if you do, buy a used car. The 160,000 miles I put on my 2008 Saturn VUE helped me tremendously. It survived long enough for me to pay off a significant portion of my debt and save up for a down payment on another used car to take its place.

Keep Doing the Things That Feed Your Soul: I did a lot of writing while I was broke. Don't get it twisted; being broke did not make me a better writer. I wrote to take my mind off my dire situation and give me a sense of control. When I was writing, I worried less. I was creating more, and it gave me hope that I could write myself out of my situation.

Accept Help When Given: Some of my friends could tell I was struggling. They never came right out and said it, but they knew. They offered help in small and large ways like paying for a dinner or offering to share frequent flyer miles so I could get to a gig. Don't let your pride get in the way of friends doing what friends do.

ABOUT THE AUTHOR

Tim Stafford is a poet and educator from Lyons, IL. He is the editor of the "Learn Then Burn" anthology series (Write Bloody) and he is the author of the collection "The Patron Saint of Making Curfew" (Haymarket Books). As a former Chicago Poetry Slam Champion, he has appeared on HBO's Def Poetry Jam and at festivals throughout the US and Europe including the German National Poetry Slam, WOERDZ Festival (Switzerland), and the International Spoken Word Festival (Germany). He currently teaches at a restorative justice-based alternative high school in Cook County, IL and teaches poetry workshops all over the country. Tim currently lives in Willow Springs, IL with his partner, son, and a beagle/dachshund named Elmer.

For booking info and all things Tim, please check out
www.timstaffordwrites.com

ACKNOWLEDGMENTS

"Why We Got Kicked Out of the Taco Bell" was previously published in Taco Bell Quarterly.

"Apologies to Lübeck," was previously published in the Brimborion.

"Benediction for When My Mechanic Calls to Tell Me What is Wrong With My Car" was based on a poem by Cristin O'Keefe Aptowicz.

THANK YOU

My partner Hiu: I'm only doing this stuff because I want you to think I'm cool.

My kiddo Michael: I could not ask for a cooler kid.

Thank you to my Mom and Dad. Thank you for watching Elmer and I hope you enjoy the poems I wrote about you!

Thank you to Matt and Shannon. Don't worry, the poems about you will be in my next book.

Thank you to Derrick Brown and the Write Bloody team for believing in this book and allowing me to join the ranks of my favorite poets.

Thank you to my editors Haley Hutchinson and Adrian Wyatt for their endless patience.

Thank you to Aricka Foreman and Maya Marshall at Haymarket Books.

Thank you to Natasha Carrizosa and Judah. Trust.

Thank you to my cover artist Jourdon Gullett for your continued radness.

I hope everyone has a cheerleader like Cristin O'Keefe Aptowicz in their life. Thank you for the notes, the nudges, the pizza, and the friendship.

Thank you to Dan "Slammy Sosa" Sullivan for being the Tango to my Cash.

Thank you to Joel Chmara for keeping me writing and creating through a pandemic.
Thank you to J.W. Basilo for the hot dog hangs.

Thank you to Molly Meacham and Shelley Elaine Geiszler. Y'all were on my mind a lot throughout the entire writing process of this book.

Thank you Robbie Q Telfer for your commitment to conservation and looking weird in sportcoats.

Thank you Marc Smith for trusting me with your stage.

Thank you Corral and Crawford for talking much-needed shit before work and for helping me believe in a world beyond broke.

Thank you to the coffee shops throughout Chicago that allowed me to sit for too long to work on poems in between my day job and part-time gig, especially Ground Up Cafe (West Loop), Star Lounge (Ukrainian Village), The Brewed (Avondale), and Jackalope (Bridgeport).

In the time it took to write this book, the world lost some tremendous poets I miss terribly. Thank you to Maureen Seaton, Danny Solis, Evan "Copasetic Soul" Hlliard, Shappy Seasholtz, Cydney Edwards, Dr. Richard Prince, Duncan H.G. Mitchell, and Freddy from the Green Mill…*Goodnight Freddy*.

IF YOU LIKE TIM, TIM LIKES...

Cristin O'Keefe Aptowicz
Derrick C. Brown
Anis Mojgani
Idris Goodwin

Write Bloody Publishing publishes and promotes great books of poetry every year. We believe that poetry can change the world for the better. We are an independent press dedicated to quality literature and book design, with an office in Los Angeles, California.

We are grassroots, DIY, bootstrap believers. Pull up a good book and join the family. Support independent authors, artists, and presses.

Want to know more about Write Bloody books, authors, and events? Join our mailing list at

www.writebloody.com

WRITE BLOODY BOOKS

After the Witch Hunt — Megan Falley

Aim for the Head: An Anthology of Zombie Poetry — Rob Sturma, Editor

Allow The Light: The Lost Poems of Jack McCarthy — Jessica Lohafer, Editor

Amulet — Jason Bayani

Any Psalm You Want — Khary Jackson

Atrophy — Jackson Burgess

Birthday Girl with Possum — Brendan Constantine

The Bones Below — Sierra DeMulder

Born in the Year of the Butterfly Knife — Derrick C. Brown

Bouquet of Red Flags — Taylor Mali

Bring Down the Chandeliers — Tara Hardy

Ceremony for the Choking Ghost — Karen Finneyfrock

A Constellation of Half-Lives — Seema Reza

Counting Descent — Clint Smith

Courage: Daring Poems for Gutsy Girls — Karen Finneyfrock, Mindy Nettifee, & Rachel McKibbens, Editors

Cut to Bloom — Arhm Choi Wild

Dear Future Boyfriend — Cristin O'Keefe Aptowicz

Do Not Bring Him Water — Caitlin Scarano

Don't Smell the Floss — Matty Byloos

Drive Here and Devastate Me — Megan Falley

Drunks and Other Poems of Recovery — Jack McCarthy

The Elephant Engine High Dive Revival — Derrick C. Brown, Editor

Every Little Vanishing — Sheleen McElhinney

Everyone I Love Is a Stranger to Someone — Annelyse Gelman

Everything Is Everything — Cristin O'Keefe Aptowicz

Favorite Daughter — Nancy Huang

The Feather Room — Anis Mojgani
Floating, Brilliant, Gone — Franny Choi
Glitter in the Blood: A Poet's Manifesto for Better, Braver Writing — Mindy Nettifee
Gold That Frames the Mirror — Brandon Melendez
The Heart of a Comet — Pages D. Matam
Heavy Lead Birdsong — Ryler Dustin
Heirloom — Ashia Ajani
Here I Am Burn Me — Kimberly Nguyen
Her Whole Bright Life — Courtney LeBlanc
Hello. It Doesn't Matter. — Derrick C. Brown
Help in the Dark Season — Jacqueline Suskin
Hot Teen Slut — Cristin O'Keefe Aptowicz
How the Body Works the Dark — Derrick C. Brown
How to Love the Empty Air — Cristin O'Keefe Aptowicz
I Love Science! — Shanny Jean Maney
I Love You Is Back — Derrick C. Brown
The Importance of Being Ernest — Ernest Cline
The Incredible Sestina Anthology — Daniel Nester, Editor
In Search of Midnight — Mike McGee
In the Pockets of Small Gods — Anis Mojgani
Junkyard Ghost Revival — Derrick C. Brown, Editor
Keep Your Little Lights Alive — John-Francis Quiñonez
Kissing Oscar Wilde — Jade Sylvan
The Last American Valentine — Derrick C. Brown, Editor
The Last Time as We Are — Taylor Mali
Learn Then Burn — Tim Stafford & Derrick C. Brown, Editors
Learn Then Burn Teacher's Guide — Tim Stafford & Molly Meacham, Editors
Learn Then Burn 2: This Time It's Personal — Tim Stafford, Editor
Lessons on Being Tenderheaded — Janae Johnson

Love Ends In A Tandem Kayak — Derrick C. Brown
Love in a Time of Robot Apocalypse — David Perez
The Madness Vase — Andrea Gibson
Multiverse: An Anthology of Superhero Poetry of Superhuman Proportions — Rob Sturma & Ryk McIntyre, Editors
My, My, My, My, My — Tara Hardy
The New Clean — Jon Sands
New Shoes on a Dead Horse — Sierra DeMulder
Open Your Mouth like a Bell — Mindy Nettifee
Ordinary Cruelty — Amber Flame
Our Poison Horse — Derrick C. Brown
Over the Anvil We Stretch — Anis Mojgani
Pansy — Andrea Gibson
Pecking Order — Nicole Homer
The Pocketknife Bible — Anis Mojgani
Pole Dancing to Gospel Hymns — Andrea Gibson
Racing Hummingbirds — Jeanann Verlee
Reasons to Leave the Slaughter — Ben Clark
Redhead and the Slaughter King — Megan Falley
Rise of the Trust Fall — Mindy Nettifee
Said the Manic to the Muse — Jeanann Verlee
Scandalabra — Derrick C. Brown
Slow Dance with Sasquatch — Jeremy Radin
The Smell of Good Mud — Lauren Zuniga
Some of the Children Were Listening — Lauren Sanderson
Songs from Under the River — Anis Mojgani
Strange Light — Derrick C. Brown
The Tigers, They Let Me — Anis Mojgani
Thin Ice Olympics — Jeffery McDaniel
38 Bar Blues — C.R. Avery
This Way to the Sugar — Hieu Minh Nguyen

Time Bomb Snooze Alarm — Bucky Sinister
Uh-Oh — Derrick C. Brown
Uncontrolled Experiments in Freedom — Brian S. Ellis
The Undisputed Greatest Writer of All Time — Beau Sia
The Way We Move Through Water — Lino Anunciacion
We Will Be Shelter — Andrea Gibson, Editor
What Learning Leaves — Taylor Mali
What the Night Demands — Miles Walser
Working Class Represent — Cristin O'Keefe Aptowicz
Workin' Mime to Five — Dick Richards
Write About an Empty Birdcage — Elaina Ellis
Yarmulkes & Fitted Caps — Aaron Levy Samuels
The Year of No Mistakes — Cristin O'Keefe Aptowicz
Yesterday Won't Goodbye — Brian S. Ellis

www.ingramcontent.com/pod-product-compliance
Lightning Source LLC
Chambersburg PA
CBHW060538080526
44586CB00012B/785